NYASHA WILLIAMS AND **GRACE BANDA**

ILLUSTRATIONS BY **KIMISHKA NAIDOO**

elemental
ALCHEMIST

Andrews McMeel
PUBLISHING®

ANDREWS MCMEEL PUBLISHING
a division of Andrews McMeel Universal
1130 Walnut Street, Kansas City, Missouri 64106

www.andrewsmcmeel.com

23 24 25 26 27 RLP 10 9 8 7 6 5 4 3 2 1
ISBN: 978-1-5248-8013-2

Editor: **DANYS MARES**
Art Director/Designer: **DIANE MARSH**
Production Editor: **MARGARET UTZ**
Production Manager: **TAMARA HAUS**

ATTENTION: SCHOOLS AND BUSINESSES
Andrews McMeel books are available at quantity discounts with
bulk purchase for educational, business, or sales promotional
use. For information, please email the Andrews McMeel
Publishing Special Sales Department: sales@amuniversal.com.

dedication

FROM NYASHA—

To **MY ANCESTORS**, for
their loving guidance.

To the **ELEMENTAL SPIRITS**, for
their patience in us finding balance.

To **GRACE**, for sharing her wisdoms from
the Elements with me and in this deck.

FROM GRACE—

To **NYASHA**, for believing in me
enough to collaborate on this deck
and for her sisterly wisdom.

To **MY ANCESTORS**, for all their
wisdom, strength, and light,
and for our work together.

To the **ELEMENTAL SPIRITS**, for all
they give us to nourish and align, and
for all they gave to create this deck.

contents

DECK STORY **vi**

TAROT VS. ORACLE **vii**

PREPARING FOR A READING **viii**

ELEMENT **SPREADS** IN ARRANGEMENT **1**

SPIRIT CARD MEANINGS **9**

AIR CARD MEANINGS **21**

FIRE CARD MEANINGS **41**

EARTH CARD MEANINGS **61**

WATER CARD MEANINGS **81**

ABOUT THE AUTHORS **100**

ABOUT THE ILLUSTRATOR **102**

deck story

I brought my second-youngest sister, Grace, into collaborating on the deck with me, as I understood it was meant to be a tool rooted in the elements. My sister and I have a handful of writing projects we are building aligned with the elements, so us working together on this felt like a natural and solid decision.

Grace and I are called and connected to different elements—she is grounded in earth, and I move with the tides in water. It has been interesting watching our relationships with the elements develop and grow while building this deck, working together, and following our soul missions.

The deck focuses on the characteristics and traits of the five elements, highlighting how to balance the elements within yourself. Each element has its strengths and challenges, which we face within ourselves, in our environments—both natural and created, and through all interactions.

The elements help us understand the laws of nature and the world we live in. They have the ability to calm, feed, or destroy. We hope that this deck helps you discern what you need to add, subtract, or unearth within your internal and external equilibriums.

Much gratitude,
NYASHA & **GRACE**

TAROT vs.
oracle

Both tarot and oracle cards/decks are Divination tools used for communication and self-reflection. Each one offers insight, but the structure of the tools varies quite a bit.

Tarot decks are often based on the Rider–Waite deck, one of the original deck designs of tarot. They have a set total of 78 cards that are divided into the major (22) and minor (56) arcana. The decks have a rigid format with all decks having the same cards and figures. Tarot decks generally differ by theme or genre, such as love, culture, or animals. While the illustrations may differ between decks, the meanings of the cards remain fundamentally the same. Learning tarot takes time and practice but, once mastered, can provide a very detailed reading.

In contrast, oracle decks do not follow a framework. There is no set number of cards per deck, and the use of suits and figures are up to the author. Each oracle deck has a specific topic meant to serve a specific purpose. No two oracle decks are the same. Oracle cards don't require as much practice or learning when engaging, but interpretation requires a different level of intimacy, asking for discernment and alignment with one's intuition.

The cards can be used in combination with each other for deeper spiritual readings. Advanced readers often use multiple decks, including tarot and oracle, to enrich and engage in more complex Divination. Tarot provides deeper understanding, and oracle gives clarity and insight on next steps.

PREPARING FOR A
reading

CREATE A SACRED SPACE

Oracle cards are sacred Divination tools, and they need to be treated with respect and honor. Give them a place that is theirs to rest and be. You also need to prepare yourself and the space to use them by energetically cleansing in a way that calls to you (burning tobacco, rosemary, or palo santo, or spraying spiritual water). Remember to cleanse the deck before and after every reading.

INFUSE YOUR ENERGY INTO THE DECK

Touch your cards. Feel their edges in the palm of your hand and breathe with your deck, allowing the energy to flow between you and every single card in your hands. You and your oracle cards have a relationship, and it is through energetic touch that your deck works with you.

SHUFFLE YOUR DECK

When you feel tuned into the cards, shuffle them however feels right to you.

SUGGESTION: When you use any deck for the first time, to help build that relationship, after infusion, interview your new deck with a deck interview card spread.

CLARITY

As you shuffle, state your intention clearly. Decide what you would like guidance on and ask the deck your question. Choosing spreads can also help the deck understand your intention. With each card placement representing a question, it may give you a deeper, more complex answer.

JUMPER CARDS:

A "jumper" card is a card that flies or jumps out while shuffling. These can be either messages that your Spirit Guides need you to know in that instant, or they can be push cards—cards that are not directly a part of your reading but need to inform you of the type of energy in your reading.

PULL YOUR CARD(S) AND INTERPRET

Allow your intuition to guide where and when you pull. Sit and observe your card(s), their details, and what calls to you in the illustrations. Let your intuition help guide and connect you to what the cards mean to you. You will not always know immediately what the cards are trying to tell you, but the more you get to know the deck the easier it becomes to read. Read cards from left to right.

READ YOUR GUIDEBOOK

Sit and try to interpret before seeking answers from the guidebook because it is only there to suggest meaning for you. After considering what the cards could mean, you may read the card description and gain more understanding. It is important that you remember that the book is only a guide to help you better connect with your own intuition.

PROCESS AND CLOSE

Think about what you gained from the reading. Where have the cards led you? What will you do with what you learned? And how do you feel after your reading?

SUGGESTION: It is helpful to keep a journal to record your readings, so you can always go back, reflect, and figure out next steps based on what you have spiritually received.

REMEMBER:

Oracle cards may not always make sense to you. In this instance, do not try to force what the card may mean; the meaning may come to you later, which is another reason to keep a Divination journal. At the end of the day, it is all about your intuition—trust it and don't overthink.

element

SPREADS IN ARRANGEMENT

ELEMENTS OF LIFE SPREAD

(Five-Card Spread)

1. SPIRIT: Representing your true self

2. AIR: Representing clarity on what
you need most right now

3. FIRE: Representing manifestations

4. EARTH: Representing your environment,
internal and external

5. WATER: Representing how you communicate

SPIRIT SPREAD

(Four-Card Spread)

1. The state of your connection to spirit
2. What is limiting the connection
3. How you can tune into your intuition
4. What you need to add to your physical life to strengthen
   your inner self

AIR SPREAD

(Five-Card Spread)

1. The current state of your thoughts
2. Problems that may prevent you from focusing on your
   intentions
3. Your state of flexibility around change
4. What you can do to remove cloudiness and provide
   clarity
5. How you should welcome changes

FIRE SPREAD
(Four-Card Spread)
1. The desires and passions you have for life
2. What is holding you back from achieving those desires
3. The spark you need to create the life you want
4. How to embrace growth after these desires come to pass

EARTH SPREAD
(Five-Card Spread)
1. Current state of your roots
2. The reason you are not grounded
3. What you need to do to become grounded
4. What you need add to your daily life in order to build a relationship with the earth and your grounded self
5. The state of your mountain—how you grow after you reach the peak

WATER SPREAD
(Five-Card Spread)
1. The state of your emotions in this moment
2. What is preventing your emotions from flowing
3. What you need to release to restore fluidity
4. What positive habits you need to adopt, mentally and/or physically
5. Outcome of your emotional release

MORE
spreads

INTERVIEW YOUR NEW DECK
(SEVEN-CARD SPREAD)

1. Describe yourself
2. What is your strength as a deck?
3. What is your weakness as a deck?
4. Describe me
5. What can you teach me?
6. How can I best learn from and collaborate with you?
7. What is the potential of our relationship?

MY WELL-BEING SPREAD
(THREE-CARD SPREAD)

1. Your physical state
2. Your emotional state
3. Your spiritual state

YOUR DAILY FREQUENCY SPREAD
(THREE-CARD SPREAD)

1. Your current frequency (the energy you are releasing)
2. What you are attracting with that energy
3. How you can attract more positivity and abundance

ANCESTRAL HEALING SPREAD
(SIX-CARD SPREAD)

1. The type of relationship you have with your ancestral lineage
2. How this relationship affects your life
3. What you can do to heal your lineage
4. What this healing will look like
5. How you can remain grounded while doing this work
6. How you can honor your ancestors moving forward

HEALING YOUR INNER CHILD
(SEVEN-CARD SPREAD)

1. How your inner child feels currently
2. What you lacked as a child
3. Something that left your inner child scarred
4. How that is affecting your life now
5. Something you can do to heal your inner child
6. How you can support your inner child
7. A message from your inner child

READ YOUR CHAKRAS
(SEVEN-CARD SPREAD)

ROOT: Where you need grounding, foundation

SACRAL: Your pleasure and emotion balance

SOLAR PLEXUS: Work, control, and confidence

HEART: Relationships and self-love, forgiveness

THROAT: Your authentic self and communication

THIRD EYE: Intuition, ancestors, Spirit Guides

CROWN CHAKRA: Your connection to your higher self

THE
elements

The elements are the physical composition of human life: air, fire, earth, and water. Each element helps us better understand the alignments, abilities, and connections of what our lives are composed of and how elements nourish us. However, nothing lives without spirit, the final element, existing in all.

SPIRIT

Spirit is universal energy, the element that thrives within every physical element. Existing within us, above us, and below us, spirit is Divinely binding: the key to harmonizing and uniting all life, as well as the connection between body and soul.

AIR

Air is masculine and is associated with the east direction. It represents intellect, communication, higher consciousness, and new beginnings and thought. The best time of day to channel air is at sunrise and seasonally in spring.

ASTROLOGICAL SIGNS RULED BY AIR: **Gemini, Libra, Aquarius**

FIRE

Fire is masculine and is associated with the south direction, often related to immense heat, opposing the north. It represents passion, renewal, courage, will, and intense purification. The best time of day to channel fire is at noon and seasonally in summer.

ASTROLOGICAL SIGNS RULED BY FIRE: Aries, Leo, Sagittarius

EARTH

Earth is feminine and is associated with the north direction, often related to the cold, opposing south. It represents grounding, hearth, health, stability, wisdom, and cycles. The best time of day to channel earth is at midnight and seasonally in winter.

ASTROLOGICAL SIGNS RULED BY EARTH: Taurus, Virgo, Capricorn

WATER

Water is feminine and is associated with the west direction. It represents intuition, emotion, spirituality, and cleansing. The best time of day to channel water is at sunset and seasonally in autumn.

ASTROLOGICAL SIGNS RULED BY WATER: Cancer, Scorpio, Pisces

spirit
CARD MEANINGS

the soul

The soul is what makes you *you*. Know that you're here on earth with a purpose, with a soul mission. Walking in that knowing is essential and critical. Much has been done to ensure that you are here now, in this moment, in this timeline, in this universe. If you are unclear about why, it is time to figure it out.

Your soul mission is aligned to what will bring the most good to yourself and to the world as a whole. A significant link in connecting you to your life's purpose is your birth (when, where, and to whom). When we are on earth, we often operate with mind, body, and soul as separate entities and medically treat them individually, but in their true and purest form, they operate in balance and support of one another.

When you intentionally quiet your loud ego, you will be able to better hear the voice of your soul.

- **What is your intuition telling you?**
- **Do you have curses here to break?**
- **Are you being called to lead, serve, or heal?**

TAKE ACTION

Turn up the volume. Close your eyes. Listen to the music of your soul.

the ancestors

the ancestors

Loved ones and those who carried your blood, who walked this earth before you, are reaching out—they want to connect. Do you hear their calls? Who better to guide you on this challenging, difficult, and enriching journey than those who hold you in their spirit and heart? Speak to them and lay your worries at their altar.

Your Ancestors are your biggest cheerleaders! Pay homage to your lineage as their sacrifices, known and unknown, have gotten you to where you are now. Work toward gracefully giving and receiving—your community extends beyond the physical realm.

• **Are you seeing the signs?**
• **When was the last time you spent time in nature?**
• **How is the health of your ancestral altar?**

TAKE ACTION

Call out to invoke ancestral veneration (speak out loud as frequently as you feel called).

Ancestors, known and unknown, who want
wealth in all its forms for me and my family.
Be with me now. Please guide me on my
path with your wisdom and guidance.

I am the root of your root, soil of your soil,
bone of your bone, and blood of your blood.

Walk with me in the commitment to
lineage and allow me to grow our legacy.

spiritual awakening

spiritual awakening

STAGES OF AN AWAKENING

THE DARK NIGHT OF SOUL: An event in your life has changed/ will change your vision of how life should be. Don't ignore the call, it is time to begin the journey to make a change.

INNER CONFLICT: You begin to doubt everything you have been learning or doing and feel the call to do differently. You continue to search for knowledge, but are feeling overwhelmed and exhausted, shadow work can do that to a person. Do not let your ego prevent you from progressing on your spiritual journey.

METAMORPHOSIS: Start to rethink your behaviors, modifying them so that you become in alignment with who you really are. You might lose interest in certain things or even gain new interests. Think more about protecting your energy alignment.

MASTERING YOUR LESSONS: Your old patterns and behaviors are starting to reappear. Don't fight it. Things are resurfacing so that you can continue to grow, make changes, and let go of what is no longer needed. It could be some unresolved issue that needs your attention or a behavior that you need to change.

TAKE ACTION

GROUNDING/BALANCE YOURSELF—look at the situation from your new perspective.

SHADOW WORK—process, feel, and release the heavy.

SPIRITUAL CLEANSING—baths and cleaning of frequented spaces.

the mother

When we care for the Mother, we give to descendants ensuring that they will have all that they need. Honoring the Mother means living in harmony with the earth and all of her spirits. The Mother is always the beginning, breathing new realities and life into the world. It is within a Mother's first heartbeat that she gives us the resources of Her body to grow and nourish our own.

The Mother carries the spirit of love, tenderness, and ferocity. She provides hard-to-swallow but necessary lessons. It is impossible to have healthy societies without healthy Mothers. Our health and quality of life are intertwined with the Mother. When we live in balance, you know that there is more than enough for all.

- **Do you ask before you take?**
- **Do you offer in return?**
- **Do you show gratitude?**

TAKE ACTION
Engage in an act of service.

the ~ divine

The Divine is universal energy, just as spirit is the universal element. You are a Divine being, with all of your flaws and your wounds, and you are exactly where you need to be at this exact moment. If you have been looking for purpose or guidance around your purpose, Divinity provides guidance in rediscovering your soul mission and anchoring you in your purpose. Too often when we are searching for higher beings to make sense of our current journey and walk, we forget that the same Divinity we are searching for is also within us.

That is not to say that our journey is without bumps in the road and additional help isn't welcome. As you work to live out your purpose and soul mission, there are Divine beings to aid and guide you. Divinity amplifies the callings within your soul. They can aid with clarity when you feel unsure about what is next or lost on your path. This card carries the powerful energetic charge of asking. Speak your heart and worries to the universe and be open to what the universe sends your way.

- **When was the last time you spoke to the trees?**
- **What is your mission on Earth, and which deity works in that same realm?**
- **Are you open to sharing your wants, needs, and dreams with the Divine?**

TAKE ACTION

Go to a place in nature that calls to you and share whatever you carry, heart and soul. Ask for wisdom toward moving in alignment with your highest good and with ease.

air
CARD MEANINGS

goddess of the east

It is only when we walk in our truth that we herald a new beginning, like how the sun rises at the beginning of each day. Something new will arrive, and you should welcome it courageously, without fear, anxiety, or doubt. Air carries the intellect needed to survive whatever is thrown your way.

Air holds space for seeking prosperity and welcoming knowledge to build new, innovative ideas. Oya is the Orisha of the winds and storms. She comes with chaotic and destructive change, but it is necessary for new growth. Understand that what she destroys, you no longer need.

- **If you had to list the things you love, how long would it take for you to list yourself?**
- **Who are you when you are bare?**
- **What have you outgrown that you are continuing to wear?**

TAKE ACTION

Let go of any and all that is preventing you from shedding your skin.

TRY
something
NEW

knowledge

When looking to grow spiritually, the tendency to rush to seek information for clarity and understanding is second nature. If you are the first in your family to begin ascending or walking the path of Ancestral Veneration, it can be hard to know where to begin. There are rules, especially for Black and Indigenous people of color, that are specific to you, your lineage, energy, and soul.

You cannot look outside yourself and your knowing for the answers. Do not give others access to your Ancestors and Spirit Guides for information that is available to you once you tap in. This means aligning your inner moral compass and your intuition to allow you to better hear yourself. Your intuition carries the memories, wisdom, and knowledge of all of those connected to your line before you. Learn to trust yourself and your discernment, and the answers will appear as you are ready.

- Do you listen to your gut?
- How does your intuition speak to you (visuals, thoughts, feelings, emotions)?
- Are you in alignment with your values?

TAKE ACTION

Create a date with yourself and mark it on your calendar. (Allow the freedom and flexibility of at least three hours, if not all day.)

When the time comes, get in your car and drive (or walk) without knowing where you are going. Allow the experience to unfold without the concern of time.

intuition

You are intuitive. Pause for a beat and listen to how Spirit communes with you. Do you have an inner sense of knowing? Are you guided by physical sight or seeing in your mind's eye? Can you hear knowledge and truth? Do you emotionally or physically receive messages? This is your sign to work on strengthening the pathway that naturally communes to you, providing Ancestral wisdom, counsel from your higher self, and enlightenment from the Universe.

A huge part of growing in your spiritual walk is to strengthen the gateway to lineage consciousness. Let this heart awareness operate as an inner compass and your most reliable guide. Spirit asks you to make time for the element that calls to your soul and is part of your core. Unite with that element and listen with your senses. It is time to open new doors and windows in your mind. Being linked to your intuition will help build your internal traffic light.

- Do you turn to others for answers you already have inside of you?
- Do you use both your spiritual and physical senses?
- Who is louder: your intuition or your ego?

TAKE ACTION

Make decisions based on love, compassion, hope, peace, honesty, and grace (from your intuition), not based on fear, judgment, greed, inconsistency, or scarcity.

renewal

It is time to re-indigenize. This means remembering your commitment to yourself, the world community, and the earth. Remember your relationship with yourself. Remember your relationships with all living things and the land. Remember you are in a relationship with others. Remember and know you and others are whole and enough. Remember to walk in abundance and wealth, knowing the riches of your culture, roots, traditions, history, and creativity. Remember to continue to build and maintain regenerative systems and partnerships with others and the planet.

Renewal is a call to reconnect to yourself, your body, and your energy. Listen to your best friend (your body) and ask what it needs. So many of us give to the world and others through our jobs, careers, and pure passion. That takes a lot of heart energy. Make sure to not give from your core but from the overflow.

TAKE ACTION

Spend some time in a body of water.

change

Remember when you were wishing and working toward what you have now? None of your milestones would (and shall) come about without change. Every spiritual awakening and walk calls for growth, healing, and faith allowing us to develop, evolve, and expand. Just like a caterpillar knows when it has outgrown a stage in its life and it is time to move forward, learn to gain that same discernment.

Understand nothing is forever and not all things that come into your life are meant to be long-term. Redirection, rejection, and denial are often much appreciated in hindsight. It takes time and wisdom to appreciate Spirit closing doors and bucketloads of belief that new pathways will come to light.

- **Do you fear the truth?**
- **Can you be comfortable in the vulnerable?**
- **Do you fear the results if they are not your expected or planned outcome?**

TAKE ACTION

Build a new positive habit and sustain it for a month.

dishonesty

Dishonesty is rooted in fear. The fear is rooted in insecurity, avoidance, vulnerability, and control. Lies, no matter how "white" (racial programming) or "insignificant" they may seem, breed disloyalty. Whether you are lying, to yourself or others, or someone is being dishonest with you, a secret is at hand. The secret is given power and weight by the act of concealing it. Accumulated falsehoods and deception can show their impact on your health (mentally, physically, spiritually, and emotionally).

Be wary of people, spaces, and jobs/professions/careers that encourage fabrications and do not call you out when you fib. While it can feel easier to defend one's actions than honestly examine them, know that admissions require courage. Step out from behind the deceitful smoke screen we tend to lean on to justify being misleading. Being candid and genuine immensely raises personal and collective vibrations, allowing us to, more accurately, reflect and grow truthfully in our identity.

- Do your words and actions match and conspire in alignment?
- Do you engage with others and enter spaces as all of you? Or only show parts of the whole?
- Do you really know what the outcome will be if you are truthful?

TAKE ACTION

Make decisions based on what you truly think and feel. Own up to and only commit to what you really want to do.

touchy

touchy

Spirit says, "Take a chill pill." This card symbolizes reactive interactions. Pay conscious attention to your thoughts and engagements with others and how others are choosing to engage with you. Being harsh with your words and having no patience or grace or compassion are all commutative red flags. They are all linked to overreacting and being impulsive. When we act instinctively, we act through an altered sense of perception. We are unable to see the situation for what it is because of the emotional surge, often linked to past trauma, causing us to react.

Slow down to be conscious about not allowing your defenses and emotions to be the driving force of your decision-making and behavior. Pause to understand and root out your triggers and allow yourself to hear what is being said without the lens of your thoughts, biases, and emotions clouding the way.

- In what situations do I respond differently than I would like?
- How important is this to me? (How will I feel about it tomorrow? In a week? In five years?)
- In addition to concentrating on my message, how can I phrase things so that I am properly understood?

TAKE ACTION
Seek professional guidance to help you see your thoughts and actions outside of your own head.

fickle

fickle

Bring some Earth energy into your life. When you are unsure about what is next, struggle to make decisions, and have the feeling of operating aimlessly, it is time to ground. Grounding or Earthing is a physical reconnecting, it is you allowing your energy to fuse with the healing energy of nature. As woo-woo as it may sound, grounding is scientific. Choosing to actively make contact with the soil allows us to discharge energy and recharge, realigning our electrical energy and enabling us to heal at the cellular level.

This healing opens up space for feeling focused, clear, and centered. When we are ungrounded, we are no different than an item floating in the breeze, going whichever way the wind blows. It is an unbalanced state of being. Being disjointed also hints at the need to make space for shadow work that you may be avoiding. When you re-root yourself, you can stand tall and firm in your energy, being less influenced by anything working to stray you off your path.

- **What haven't you admitted out loud yet?**
- **Are you focusing on the past, present, or future?**
- **What is your hope rooted in?**

TAKE ACTION

Get physical. Outside (hiking, camping, gardening, daydreaming, swimming). Do any physical activity that calls to you while being disconnected from any tech.

inconsistent

Manifesting and following "The Secret" has become second nature to many today. What is forgotten or left out of building the life of your dreams and a strong base for living out your soul mission is discipline. Spiritual discipline. These are the practices, habits, and rituals that work to strengthen your bond to Spirit, helping train the soul and open the way for true liberation. Hearing the call to tap into your spirituality is the beginning, but gaining confidence and results in your spiritual walk requires steadfast determination.

Being immersed spiritually requires consistency and effort, otherwise it will fall flat, similar to the erratic watering of plants. Your relationship with discipline shows your relationship with time. You must dedicate time and energy for any pursuit to flourish. Build spiritual stability into your daily routine. Being disciplined is the ultimate showcasing of self-love because acts of discipline show belief and faith in yourself, others, and Spirit.

- Do you know that what you don't do is just as important as what you do?
- Who is really in control of you and your time currently?
- Do you finish what you start?

TAKE ACTION
Choose to challenge your own excuses.

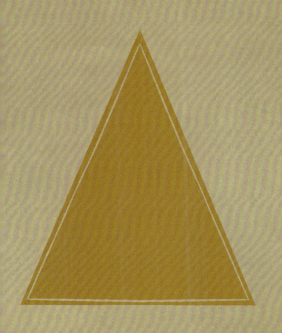

fire

CARD MEANINGS

goddess of the south

It is time to go on a quest, and in that walk, you will face the unknown of the south. Now, in the present, is the time to make your position known to self, for as you embark on a new adventure, you will need knowledge, passion, and wanderlust to fill your hungry heart. Take a chance; fire is on your side to protect you fiercely on your quest.

In fire, one is reborn like a phoenix rising from the ashes, daring to fly higher than ever before. Motivation, self-assertion, and courage are tools to help you push forward into the unknown. Morimi is the Yoruba Goddess of Fire. She invokes the flame to prepare you for new planting in your life, purifying you in fire. So take that risk you have been dying to take—the flame has been lit!

- **What old habit needs to be burned for you to face your journey fiercely?**
- **Do you have a bucket list? If so, how many things have you completed?**
- **Do you only want to try something new when with others?**

TAKE ACTION
Do something you have always wanted to do but never have.

SAY
yes
MORE OFTEN

passion

Ignition . . . Your soul is set ablaze unexpectedly, bursting with energy from feeling the power of an intense, compelling desire for something or someone. Lean in to focused energy. Like fire, passion can consume wildly if left untamed. You cannot allow yourself to be devoured by the flame of passion. Instead, drink it in, contemplate it, and consider what action will ignite you.

Observe your own behavior when in the throes of zeal. Are you focused or lost in the intensity? This is the sign of the flame that will burn you or enhance you. Listen to your body, listen to your soul, and listen to what they cry out for. This is your call to walk boldly into passion. Vitality, energy, and power are in this card; use this to your advantage. Allow the mind, the soul, and spirit to ignite you, bringing you into a new sense of life.

• **What is the last thing you did that made you feel alive?**
• **Are you afraid of what you love?**
• **What are you called to when you think of passion?**

TAKE ACTION

Take a risk . . . with the possibility of being consumed and the focus to avoid it. Allow yourself to pursue what you love.

inspiration/creativity

inspiration / creativity

Creativity is the want of self-expression, and this want takes commitment and focus to reach completion. You have to want it and dream of it to invite it. In your own journey, creativity will come to you in many forms. It is a vessel within yourself to transport you to your higher self, and with this inspiration, there is limitless energy for creation.

Transformation is inevitable with dedication and discipline to your creative pursuit by finding the correct tools and connecting to your power. All energies thrive under certain conditions, and creativity is no different. Whatever you are envisioning will become a reality, as that is what creation is about. What you sculpt will become the product of self-expression, so be diligent but willing to take risks.

- **When was the last time you created something?**
- **How easily do you get distracted?**
- **What inspires you to use your imagination?**

TAKE ACTION

Challenge yourself to create. Think about what it teaches you about yourself and how deeply it connects you to the environment around you, physically and spiritually.

daring/courageous

The time to take action is now, for new possibilities are being forged in the flames of creation. Be hungry for adventure; create purpose and meaning in something that both scares and strengthens you. This will take confidence, discipline, and action. Stepping into the unknown requires the courage to follow through.

Be available to ask deep questions about your desires and goals. Possibilities will not be revealed to you if you are disconnected and uncommitted to yourself first. You are inevitably going to encounter other energies that will test your dedication and courage, because being afraid is often the easier route. Dare yourself to be brave and step toward truly being free.

- **How do you serve yourself?**
- **When was the last time you did something spontaneously?**
- **Are your limits your own? Have you re-evaluated your limits based on who you are now?**

TAKE ACTION

Try something out of your comfort zone.

protection

The universe, your Ancestors, your Spirit Guides, all have your back. So many before you endured and stood strong only by love and togetherness. Know you are loved and you are never alone. They protect with a powerful love, and love you not because of what you bring to the table, but because of who you are. You are asked to remember your fiery fierceness to fight for more, to fight for the future, so they may always be protected.

Do not forget it is your immediate duty to be self-aware in order to protect your whole self—mind, body, spirit, and soul. Your boundaries must be firm and your own. It is all up to you what energies you allow into your life. Examine yourself and tune into what you need to do to feel protected. Being aware of what triggers you and figuring out what the triggers are rooted in can help you better protect yourself. Your body is your best friend, always giving you a better understanding of what energies you should or shouldn't be surrounding yourself with or engaging with.

- **Do you engage in routine spiritual cleansing?**
- **Are you aware that known and unknown guides have your best interest?**
- **Do you know that there are different types of boundaries?**

TAKE ACTION

Know that it is okay to seek comfort from those who love you when you feel vulnerable.

Create a safe space where you can go to reenergize yourself and be at ease.

urge to destroy violence

A warning for you may become the target of that destructive urge. Oftentimes, this urge arises in anger, hurt, stagnancy, and times when you don't feel in control. It is human nature; however, it becomes negative and unhealthy to act on that urge impulsively instead of taking a moment to think, digest, and channel this urge into defending or creating. Giving in to the urge to destroy will invite unavoidable chaos into your life; nothing will ever be the same.

Keep in mind that in order to build and create, you must have a strong foundation. That is why ancestral healing is so important. The foundation of who you are includes those who came before you, and the future is built on the foundation of the past. It is also important to remember that the intention behind the thought matters most. Destruction for gain takes from others, and destruction for creation builds for others.

- **Have you been feeling self-doubt?**
- **Do you have any grudges against anyone, including yourself?**
- **What is the strength of your emotional foundation?**

TAKE ACTION

Engage with paper (writing, drawing, coloring).

irritable

Slow down. You are creating unnecessary panic for yourself and those around you. As soon as you feel irritation, stop and examine what it is that is affecting you. It feels the way it does because it is trying to get your attention. This feeling is a tool to guide you in where you need alignment, reevaluation, and change.

The side effects of your irritation affect those around you negatively, dishonoring the journey of others by having no patience for them. To address this, ask questions and start clearing feelings about the root of your irritation. The golden rule: focus on balance. Your interactions with others keep you in constant energetic exchange, positive and negative. It is okay to be assertive, but be kind. Grace, for yourself and others, is necessary.

- **Are your expectations reasonable?**
- **Do you suffer from stress and anxiety?**
- **In what ways do you practice empathy?**

TAKE ACTION

Do an activity that you don't enjoy with someone you love. Challenge yourself with a difficult puzzle.

anger

Heavy emotions are being felt, and they can be extremely hard to let go of. To feel anger is healthy but, just like any emotion, it needs to flow through you and be released. Every feeling is capable of creation, and anger is forged in the element of fire. You need temperament and emotional intelligence to survive the flames of your emotions.

External forces may be at play. Protect yourself from energies that do not have your best interests at heart, and do not allow them to control you. Choose your battles wisely. Protection is often wiser than a counterattack. Tune in to other elements to help balance your fire and channel it into something in harmony with your higher self. Your anger toward anything or anyone is telling you to address your true thoughts and feelings cordially to prevent all from burning out of control. Slow down and allow your mind to tell you what you need to calmly navigate this fiery time.

- **Are there thoughts and feelings you have been containing and not sharing?**
- **What do you do to help you calm down and think?**
- **What is your first response when feeling angry?**

TAKE ACTION

Cordially express your true thoughts and feelings.

WATER: Take a calming bath, preferably a spiritual bath, to wash away negative energies that may have attached themselves to you.

AIR: Take a deep breath, slow down, and temper.

EARTH: Take a moment with a tree and journal.

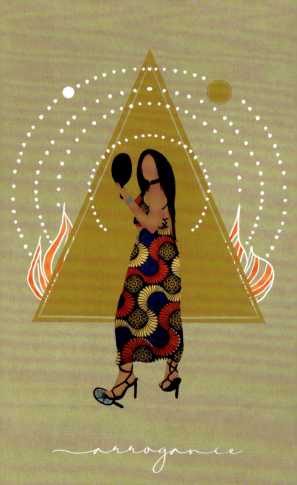

arrogance

arrogance

Arrogance is fear-based and works as a disguise that signals insecurities and a false belief of superiority. You are being called to reflect on your behavior, redirecting from an outward to inward focus. Often arrogance operates as a defense mechanism along with the desire to be seen. Make the active choice to accept and be comfortable with yourself, your path, and your abilities. Your walk and journey are your own and cannot be compared with or rated against anyone else's.

Know that perfection is an unattainable facade and make peace with life being a continual space to grow. You will make mistakes, and you will not always know the answer; respond with honesty and take accountability for your decisions. Our evolution is reliant on insights, guidance, experiences, observations, and interactions with others. Understand how others impact your walk and credit them. Step in humility, as there is always more to learn.

- Do you see others as equals or competitors?
- How do you react when others don't share your worldview?
- Are you good at being corrected lovingly by others?

TAKE ACTION

When communicating, reflect on the following:

- What are you assuming right now?
- Are you speaking with the desire to be seen or the desire to be heard?
- Are you pulling others up in conversation or are you trying to bring or keep them down?

earth
CARD MEANINGS

goddess of the north

Prepare yourself, the north is a cold and dark place. It is time to grow and make room for enlightenment and expansion. Trust yourself to know what you need to overcome the obstacles that come with the cooler climate. Take this time to plan your actions for the spring: weeding your garden, then preparing to plant your next step in the Earth, letting your seeds develop into a new bounty. Earth carries adaptability and creativity and, with it, you will feel the need to expand.

North represents introspection. Invite great wisdom and great thought into what comes next in your growth and journey. As right and true as true north is, you need to be just as sure about grounding yourself and preparing for the active changes your introspection will bring. You are at a point of endless possibility and boundless potential for something great. Take care to follow through.

- **What have you put off that needs to be done?**
- **Where do you see yourself in the next phase of your life?**
- **When was the last time you decluttered your space?**

TAKE ACTION
Learn something new about yourself and your true path and put it into action.

CHALLENGE YOURSELF TO
create

fertility

The seed of life came from the Divine Mother and, from her womb, abundant creation. In creation, the goal is to manifest balance. It is time to root yourself with the elements. Within you grows abundant potential for creation, and the only tools you need are compassion and grace toward yourself and what you are growing. Your creation becomes your responsibility, so it is important to love yourself in order to love what you are growing in the lush garden of life.

The earth is most abundantly in your favor. Fertility is our Feminine Mother. This is the time for you to bloom and allow yourself to enjoy what you currently have, what you are growing, and what it will become. Though you have the seeds of potential, they can also sprout into uncertainty and anxiety if not given the tender love and safety a mother provides. To feed the fetus, you must first feed yourself.

- **Do you know that health is generational wealth?**
- **When was the last time you took a walk?**
- **Are you listening to what your body needs?**

TAKE ACTION

Get an item made of rose quartz to wear or keep at your bedside.
Spend some time in nature.

wealth|abundance

Take a breath and be patient. You are exactly where you need to be to acquire abundance, and it is important to have faith in yourself and the Universe. Abundance is within you, and it will tailor to the thoughts and intentions of your mind and soul. The goal is set, now step into action. Gratitude attracts new opportunities into your life, while a scarcity mindset or worry of lack will magnify your fear, not allowing progress.

This is also the time to give rather than take, focusing on what you have with reflection and appreciation. Believe that there are enough resources for everyone. Be humble in your abundance and stay grounded. Take the time to affirm the goodness in your life, and honor it. Avoid impatience and a need for immediate gratification. You are limiting your wealth and abundance while on the cusp of prosperity. Divine timing is knowing that everything happens as it should.

- **Are you practicing gratitude regularly?**
- **Do you trust the Universe will always provide?**
- **What is the first thing you think of when you wake up?**

TAKE ACTION

Do something for someone and expect nothing in return.

wisdom

Wisdom, particularly self-wisdom, is not just about knowing what's best for you, but putting that knowledge into practice in your life. When you do that, the beginning of all astuteness follows. Be aware that wisdom and knowledge are not the same. Anyone is capable of acquiring data, but it is knowing what and how to apply it that matters most. If you want what's best for your soul, it starts with making the decision to have it, and not choosing is the opposite of wisdom.

While knowing yourself is an important factor of perceptiveness, insight is also about strong intuition and self-reflection. Being brave, becoming sage, is its own journey, and in stillness, the veil is lifted to many truths that may be hard to learn, but they equip you for spiritual evolution. Being blind to this opportunity is unwise and ignorant. Open your mind and welcome solitude for the better.

- What is the last thing you read?
- How easily do you set self-protective boundaries?
- Can you think of a lesson you learned from observing rather than experiencing?

TAKE ACTION

Learn from your mistakes: Being wise isn't about knowledge, it's about application.

Choose wisdom daily: No one in the world knows everything, and that is why every day is an opportunity to choose wisdom.

strength/stability

We are all one with the Earth as it is with us. Being grounded, rooted, and self-reliant during this time are important, because not having a strong foundation in who you are leads to an imbalance between yourself and your Divine connection to the Earth. As you grow, your traditions and roots can and will grow with you.

Remember, you are a tree standing tall, rooted in the Earth, because you are working hard to overcome the harsh conditions that come with life. Honor yourself, your strength, and your name. Strength comes from within you: from those who came before you, those who had the courage to fight, and those who want you to be able to do what they were unable to do. The seeds from your thoughts will flourish in soil that has been nourished by all that connects you to the Earth. Claim your choices and make sure they are rooted in your heart. Trust them, as these are your tools to build generations of wealth.

- **Do you ask for help when you need it?**
- **Are there any family traditions that resonate with you? Are there any that need to change?**
- **What fuels your desire to succeed?**

TAKE ACTION

Write down all you still have to overcome, have overcome already, and what it taught you about yourself.

superficial

superficial

You are acting like someone you are not, putting up an appearance and hoping to make it through. There is a difference between the mask and the face beneath it, and balancing both is becoming exhausting. The mask is who you present yourself as to the world, and the face is your real self. Your shadow self is part of your real self, and not embracing it as part of you will stop you from reaching your full potential. Your whole self just wants to be loved. Spirit asks, what are you hiding from the world that doesn't want to be ignored, but processed and accepted? Why don't you think your whole self has a place in this world?

By owning your truth and who you are, you can grow into who you want to be. Shed the idea or aim for perfection. Every day is a new opportunity to make a new choice, a choice for you to become better. We become who we are by what we have been exposed to and how we choose to transform and evolve. Life is about becoming your best self, not a perfect self, despite what you have endured.

- Are you aware of what triggers you?
- Think about what you have heard about perfection. Does this idea, in any way, resonate or serve you?
- Do you remember to be gentle toward yourself?

TAKE ACTION

Confront your shadow self. Begin a shadow work journal.

scornful

Changes need to be made. You will not progress in your true path with the same attitude of disdain. There are negative feelings that you are carrying and they are spreading through your life like venom in your body. Pause to figure out the root of your pain, the negativity that you are harboring, as it is standing between you and where you want to be.

It is time for reflection. Adjustments must be made to align oneself, removing any blockages from your path. There most certainly is something new and exciting around the corner, and it requires you to work through your situation and those involved. Every thought has unbound potential to harm or nurture.

• Do you have toxic thoughts that need to be released?
• Is there anything you have recently judged harshly?
• What emotions stand between you and your goals?

TAKE ACTION

Reevaluate the position you are in. Now think about why you feel the way that you do toward your position and how it is affecting your energy.

cumbersome

The weight you are carrying is making you stagnant, and it will get heavier with time until you put it down or it slips out of your hands. The load that no longer serves you, the load that does not belong to you, the load that is hard to abandon: Feel it, understand it, and then set yourself free from any cumbersome burdens.

You may feel as though you're in control, but you are using too much energy holding and managing all of that weight. This is the call to use what you have learned to restore balance within yourself. It is your responsibility to trust yourself in knowing what will liberate you, because not all is yours to sustain. When you make the space, the lessons you need to learn will then be revealed.

- **What comes to your mind about yourself when you think of** *heavy?*
- **What scares you the most about yourself?**
- **What do you do when you are stressed or anxious?**

TAKE ACTION

Confront the burdens you are carrying and evaluate them. Decide what it is you have room to carry and set those boundaries in your life.

lack of conscience

You are losing track of what is important in life. The balance in your morality is suffering due to recent decisions you may have made. You are being called out for being selfish somewhere in your life. Be more empathetic toward others and practice empathy. Life is about more than just yourself. Honor that your energy and actions affect others as well as yourself.

Alternatively, this is the call to set boundaries. Someone may be preying on you. Be wary of giving too much from your own cup to others around you. This is why a balance between selfishness and selflessness is required. It is important to give from what is overflowing and not from your own cup. Beware of possible energy vampires, who depend on empaths to give unending assistance, resources, and validation. Guard your energy from them, but keep in mind that there are others lightworking, just like you, and after taking care of yourself, make room for others too.

- **Do you act differently toward people to their face?**
- **Are you listening to your body's reaction to your actions?**
- **When was the last time you reexamined your priorities?**

TAKE ACTION

Write about what kind of person you want to be, why it is important to you, and what you need to do to become that person.

water
CARD MEANINGS

goddess of the west

Water is life, as it is essential to all. The liquid carries with it imprints of our ancestral DNA; it is the sacred blood of our first Mother. The west brings forth the energy of Divine knowledge, movement, and the psyche. This is the wisdom held by our Ancestors, Elders, midwives, and doulas. They understand the significance of this thread that connects us to the cycles of time, our environment, and the spiritual realm. Without water, there is no life.

While water is nurturing and gentle, do not mistake its traits for weakness. The tsunami and puddle are molded from the same element. Allow the flow of compassion, grace, and understanding to enter your internal rhythm, and extend that overflow to others. When you are longing to connect with the element, sing in a body of natural waters or hold a shell to your ear. Foresight given by her is to be flexible as shifts are a certainty. Just as the ocean is constantly ebbing and flowing, change is ever-present.

- **Do you know where you begin and others end?**
- **How are you making sure your cup is routinely being filled?**
- **Do you imagine a life flow in which there is balance and enough for everyone?**

TAKE ACTION

Tap into/link up with some maternal wisdom.

TAKE A

risk

healing

Spiritual healing is the effort and experience of reviving, balancing, and mending the soul. As we undergo life, we face challenges that, more often than not, leave behind trauma. We also carry generational trauma that is stored in our DNA. The modern route to handling trauma is through pharmaceuticals that encourage people to continue on with life at the same pace. Medicine is not inherently bad but is not doing any good if used as a bandage rather than getting to the root of the problem. Trauma responses are a sign to slow down, as your body is signaling that something is wrong.

Our chaotic world leaves little room for processing, taking time for your health (mental, physical, emotional, spiritual), or maintaining a sustainable work-life balance. Many people use work as an excuse not to address harmful past trials or present issues. Rest is necessary, as is taking time to face, acknowledge, and work through the difficulties and hardships we experience. Authentic healing is working to get your soul back to when it was the most you—when you knew you were safe, interacted with all in love, and joy came as easy as breathing. Do the shadow work. Our healing is necessary for the health of our world and future generations.

- What limiting beliefs have you outgrown that need transforming?
- How can you share and give love today?
- What can you do today that you didn't think you could do a year ago?

TAKE ACTION
Write a letter to your inner child.

expression

In order to speak freely, you need to live authentically. Living authentically requires being vulnerable and transparent. You must accept and love all of you, even the parts you fear to look at in the shadows. In finding your voice, take the focus off winning or being correct. Truth, responsibility, and clarity come from the heart. Unblock your vishuddha chakra! Get rid of the lump in your throat so you can confidently make choices toward expressing and defending yourself, your communities, and the world.

While society and its current systems rely on you not seeing your worth, this is your reminder to rebel. Let go of all habits planted in doubt. The trouble with expressing ourselves is linked to deflated self-esteem and lack of self-love. Walk back into knowing the weight in your voice and magic. Your voice carries narratives yet to be told. Ground yourself to hear your way clearly!

- **Do you know the power of your voice?**
- **How are you advocating for others and yourself?**
- **When was the last time you spoke your truth and felt heard, respected, and listened to?**

TAKE ACTION

Write an affirmation or a mantra to begin reciting to start your mornings.

peace

Happiness starts with being conscious of what you are placing your focus on. What you picture has so much power and can manifest. Most of life is spent searching: searching for joy, and happiness in all the wrong places, getting distracted by the goal of peace. It comes far too easy to conjure the negative. Slow down to be able to see what is already sprouting and what more you can plant to grow. While there is no one answer that fits all challenging circumstances, the struggle can appear more permanent than it really is.

Once you come to accept that reality, you can settle into your wabi-sabi. The Japanese lifestyle concept is anchored in finding beauty in imperfection and embracing a more natural form of life. It encourages us to understand that all are imperfect, incomplete, and momentary. Any pursuit of perfection or immense material gain is a matrix red herring. Wabi-sabi suggests finding peace in the imperfections and rawness of human existence. Let philosophy enrich your sense of what matters, what matters aesthetically and what matters in the realm of accomplishment.

- **Do relationships that are over or objects you no longer have continue to occupy your mind?**
- **Do you really know the difference between needs and wants?**
- **Do you physically or digitally aim to "keep up with the Joneses"?**

TAKE ACTION
Commit to thirty days of gratitude.

compassion

Compassion can be learned and cultivated, even in adulthood. We live in a world where physical and material achievements reign on high. Being tender and empathetic are practices not always paraded, though they are valued by many of the world's current systems and institutions. Acknowledge that capitalism, white supremacy, and the patriarchy foundationally stand on lies. These institutions justify themselves when given the power to oversee the narrative of pain.

There is no shame in understanding another's plight and having the desire to aid in lessening that burden or suffering. Humanitarians, zoophilists, and environmentalists do not have a soul mission of the fainthearted. Why is it too much to imagine and believe in nurturant, intersectional, and comprehensive systems, institutions, and hearts? The American dream and manifest destiny believe in colonial success and progress at the loss of others. In order for heart-based systems to flourish, we, as a global community, must invigorate collective empathy and vulnerability.

- **What is your masculine protecting your feminine from?**
- **How emotionally available are you to yourself?**
- **When you use your imagination, where do you see defaults?**

TAKE ACTION

Ask both yourself and others, what does liberation look like to you?

indifference

As a spiritual being living a human experience, remember that your core is heart-centered. Pain and trauma can have us turn to indifference as a defense mechanism. It can stem from buying into systems that value life and the humanity of some but not all. Indifference presents itself through acting cold, unmotivated, passionless, and uninterested. Once you disconnect, you begin aligning with detachment and separation. It is the acceptance of dissociating that cultivates much of our anguish.

Indifference is violent and harmful, especially when your neighbors' well-being is of no consequence to you. Apathy is a lack of response. Reasonably all individuals have experienced joy, fear, pain, sadness, disgust, and surprise. To bridge with others, push past artificial gaps and honor humanity. If we choose to deny humanity in others, we ultimately deny it in ourselves.

- **Where are you rejecting your ability to take action?**
- **Do you take time to reflect on the ways in which the perspectives of those writing history shape the history that they produce?**
- **What are you avoiding processing or feeling?**

TAKE ACTION

Ask for help and seek out professional counsel and support.

laziness

Find a rhythm and flow in making time for work, rest, and leisure in your life. This balance comes in decolonizing time itself. This means radically readjusting your expectations around yourself and others. Burnout and not being able to fully engage in space/work/relationships comes from not knowing what you need to protect your time and energy in a space. You need to set firm boundaries no matter what field you are in, as you are more than your work and the role you are expected to play in capitalism.

It is time to reimagine what it means to be valuable and productive. Amend and transform your understanding and relationships to rest, money, work, land, fellow humans, and self. Capitalism is a parasitic structure that has violently attempted to erase all Indigenous traditions and ways of life. You need to re-embrace and restructure your current lifestyle for a regenerative and sustainable way of life.

- **What do you know about the Indigenous people whose land you are currently occupying?**
- **How do you determine and measure your worth?**
- **Are you staying true to your values and making sure your needs are being met?**

TAKE ACTION

Do one thing every day that you would choose to do if you weren't working.

instability

To be completely healthy, you must take care of all aspects of your health: physical, spiritual, intellectual, social, environmental, occupational, and emotional. All must be nurtured with the understanding that none is separate from the others in finding total wellness. Most ancient civilizations believed that all parts of health, as intangible as they may seem, have a physical presence and impact. Our wellness can be compromised by a lack of support, trauma, negative-thinking habits, and chronic substance use.

Brain (mental) health is everyday health. Regular checkups in all aspects of health must be normalized and as casual as any physical annual checkup. With daily wear and tear, just like our bodies, brains need love and bandages, too. A big step toward honoring all parts of your health is giving yourself grace and compassion and extending that same compassion and grace to others.

- **Does your energy exertion match your energy receival?**
- **When was the last time you moved your body with intention?**
- **Are you fighting or inviting life?**

TAKE ACTION

Evaluate your health and wellness. List where you are admirably taking care of you and areas of wellness that need more attention.

rigidity

Consider how flexible you were growing up, not just physically but in all forms of wellness, especially mentally and physically. As we age, we become more and more rigid in our ways. Many of us regress in life, moving further and further away from our true, authentic, whole, and fluid selves to match what we think the world expects us to be. We walk away from our passions for a stable job. We repress our truth and emotions to appear easygoing and as having everything under control.

The root of your spiritual walk here on earth is rediscovering you. Remember your most healed, loved, and loving self. You need to build a space in which that version of you is safe and can enjoy life again. This is the ask of the universe: Release the parts of you that you have trapped, hidden away, and others dictated that you needed to conceal. You and all of you are needed just as you arrived on earth. Step back into your power and awaken all of you.

- Do you feel safe and whole in who you are now?
- Can you be brave?
- What is blocking you from taking the leap you keep being called to take?

TAKE ACTION

Play. Have some nostalgic "be back before the streetlights come on" kind of enjoyment.

ABOUT THE
authors

GRACE BANDA is a South African storyteller and herbalist who understands the power of stories in her culture and hopes to craft meaningful tales that can recreate and reimagine a new world.

Grace has never lost her love of stories. She grew up surrounded by Gauteng's vibrant culture and energy, and she's used those experiences to fuel her imagination and create stories that share her passion for her homeland. She believes in the power of story to shape the way we see the world, and she's been on a mission to use her voice to make a difference.

A quote that resonates with her is Audre Lorde's, "I have come to believe over and over again that what is most important to me must be spoken, made verbal and shared, even at the risk of having it bruised or misunderstood."

Because all voices are important, and everyone's story deserves to be heard, not silenced.

In addition to her writing and storytelling, Grace is also an avid herbalist and student of indigenous herbalism. She loves exploring plants' healing power and sharing her knowledge with others.

She hopes to continue sharing her work, stories, and herbalism with the world.

NYASHA WILLIAMS, a passionate social justice griot, grew up living intermittently between the United States and South Africa. Nyasha's mission is to use words and stories to decolonize literature, minds, and spiritual practices.

Nyasha is a firm believer that the story lives within each of us and that it is our mission to use stories to spread understanding, healing, and empowerment.

Nyasha's writing is rooted in her understanding of the powerful potential of stories to create transformation and reveal truths that have been hidden for too long. She strives to use her words to ignite new conversations, inspire action, and ultimately help create a more equitable and just world.

"As BIPOCs, we are operating and navigating systems that weren't made for us and are actively working against us," says Williams. "My efforts as a creator, author, and activist are to combat the systems of White supremacy, colonization, and the patriarchy, working towards decolonizing, liberating, and indigenizing our minds and world."

Her latest children's book, *Ally Baby Can: Be Feminist*, was just released, and she has five additional children's book titles coming out in 2023. She has a tarot deck, *Black Tarot: An Ancestral Awakening Deck and Guidebook*, that came out in December 2022. You can find her on Instagram at @writingtochangethenarrative. She lives in Northglenn, Colorado, with her husband.

ABOUT THE
illustrator

KIMISHKA NAIDOO is a proud South African woman of South Asian descent. With a passion for celebrating cultures, Kimishka was raised to embrace the duality of her identity and to appreciate other cultures from a young age.

The creative talent in Kimishka has led her to study film, video editing, animation, graphics design, and teaching English as a second language. She has also been fortunate enough to travel throughout Europe and Asia giving her the opportunity to learn more about the unique cultures that reside there.

Building on her cultural appreciation and creative background, Kimishka has begun to express her creativity through illustrations that highlight and amplify her appreciation for BIPOC culture and beauty.

Kimishka's mission is to encourage people to embrace the beauty of different cultures, celebrate the beauty of inclusivity, and empower people to be proud of their roots. Kimishka is a driving force for positive change, and her art is her way of sharing her message of love and acceptance with the world.